The Don't Laugh Challenge™ Joke Book

Christmas EDITION

Think YOU can win our JOKE CONTEST?!?!

The Don't Laugh Challenge is having a **CONTEST** to see who is the **MOST HILARIOUS** boy or girl in the USA.

Please have your parents email us your best **original** joke and you could win a $50 gift card to Amazon.

Here are the rules:

1. It must be funny. Please do not give us jokes that aren't funny. We get enough of those from our joke writers

2. It must be original. We have computers and we know how to use them.

3. No help from the parents. Plus, they aren't even that funny anyway!!

Email your best joke to:

Bacchuspublish@gmail.com

Winners will be announced via email.

Bacchus Publishing House

The Don't Laugh ™ Challenge Instructions:

- Sit down facing your opponent at eye level.

- Take turns reading jokes to each other.

- First person to make the opponent laugh, wins a point!

- First person to 3 points wins & is crowned The Don't Laugh MASTER.

Christmas Jokes

Why does Mrs. Claus always lay out four dishes?

Because, Santa likes the north bowl.

Why did Rudolph do so well in school?

He was the brightest student.

Why did Santa Claus eat his walking stick?

It was a candy cane.

Why do the elves write their Christmas cards in the summer?

So they're warm wishes.

What do you call a farmer in December?

A jolly rancher.

Why didn't the gift get unwrapped?

There was nobody present.

What is a mime's favorite Christmas song?

Silent Night

What did Santa say when he saw a ghost?

"Now there's the Christmas spirit!"

Why does Santa carry an umbrella?

For the "rain deer"

Where do the elves vote?

At the North Poll

What Christmas song do animals like best?

Jungle Bells

What did the man with the cold say at Christmas time?

"Sneezin's Greetings"

What did Santa ask for at the hardware store?

"Hoe Hoe Hoe"

How do Christmas trees like their ice cream?

In a pine-cone.

What reindeer wants to be an astronaut?

Comet

What do vegetables wish for at Christmas?

Peas on Earth

What does Frosty the Snowman say when he thanks you?

'Snow worries!

Did you hear about the snowman at the buffet?

He can really scarf down his food.

What did the Chihuahua say on Christmas?

Yappy Holidays!

What play gives the peanut nightmares?

The Nutcracker

What is a genie's favorite Christmas song?

We Wish You A Merry Christmas

Where did the two feet share a kiss?

Beneath the mistletoe.

Could Frosty The Snowman smell?

No, but he didn't carrot all.

What did the snowman say to the nervous squirrel?

Chill out.

What's the best kind of journal
for Christmas?

A yule-log

What's the best food on a cold night?

Chili

What's the most important for
Christmas cookies?

Mistle-dough

What do snowmen like to drink?

Frost-Tea

What did Santa say to Mrs. Claus when he looked at the clouds?

"I think it's gonna rain, dear."

Why did everyone think Rudolph was angry?

Because he was seeing red.

What did the snowflake study in geography?

A snow globe.

What did Santa name his pet fish?

Ru-dolphin

Where does Santa fly his flag?
The North Pole

Did you hear about the caterpillar who hated Christmas?
He was a grinch-worm.

What do you call an inconsiderate reindeer?
Rude-olph

What did the grumpy sheep say to the beetle on Christmas?
Bah, humbug!

Why did people kiss under the man's feet?

He had a mistle-toe

What Christmas beverage always tells you what to do?

Eggnag

Why did the beach like Christmas?

It had yule-tides

Why was Frosty always late?

Because he was a slowman.

What are the best Christmas crackers?

Nutcrackers

Why did Santa's helpers go to the gym?

For elf-improvement

Why was the Christmas gift stress-free?

He was always in the present.

What do you say underwater in December?

"Merry Fishmas"

What is it called when a polar bear tells you his feelings?

Polar Expression

What's it called when you follow an elf around?

Stocking

What do you call a mime in armor?

A silent knight

When does Santa arrive?

In the Saint Nick of time

Why did the Christmas lights quit their job?

They were burnt out.

What did the dentist call his snowman?

Flossy the Snowman.

Why did the elves trip when getting to the movies?

All of their popcorn was on a string.

How did they build Santa's workshop?

Using candy cranes.

What did Santa say when he slipped off the roof?

Fa-la-la-la-la-la-la-la-lling!

What does Santa like on his sandwiches?

Peanut butter and jolly

Why were the Christmas lights so stressed?

They were strung out.

Why did the ribbon start beatboxing?

It was covering the wrapping paper.

What do monsters like to sing at Christmas?

Scare-ols

How do fish decorate for Christmas?

With Coral Reefs

What do Christmas cookies need to sleep?

Baking sheets

What's the coldest month?

Decem-BRRR

What did the pilots have during the snowstorm?

A snowball flight

What did Santa hurt when he came into the house?

His chim-knee

What basketball team loves Christmas?

The Chicago Bells

What does the Christmas gift say during roll call?

"Present"

How does Santa shop for groceries?

By making a list and checking it twice.

What did the wolves say at Christmas?

Happy Hooooowl-idays!

What's the worst food to get in your stocking?

Coal slaw

How do Christmas presents get dressed up?

With bowties

**What does the Easter Bunny
say on Christmas?**

Merry Eggsmas!

What do you call the stinkiest elf?

Jingle Smells

**What do you call a child born
on Christmas?**

Santa Baby

**Who keeps the beat in a
Christmas band?**

The Little Drummer Boy

Why did the elf cover his bed in flour?

So he could dream of a white Christmas.

Why did Santa go for a ride on his sleigh on December 23rd?

T'was the flight before Christmas.

Why did the elves stop eating cookies?

There was a gingerbread ban.

Why did the top of the tree get to be in the play?

It was the star.

What did Scrooge say when he lost his jacket?

Brrr-humbug.

What did the chef say when he was complimented on making Christmas dinner?

'Tis the seasoning.

Why were the reindeer digging up the yard?

It was a hole-y night.

What did the baker call his favorite Christmas recipe?

The Gingerbread Plan.

What did Rudolph say when he was asked to join the ballet?

"Well, I'm no Dancer or Prancer..."

How old is Frosty?

Snow one knows.

What happens when elves run through the house?

They wreck the halls!

Who delivers gifts to animals on Christmas?

Santa Paws

What is the red-haired boys favorite dessert?

Gingerbread

How does a Christmas tree count to four?

"One, two, tree, four!"

What does Frosty The Snowman eat for dinner?

Frozen food, duh.

Why did the Christmas light go to an all-you-can-eat buffet?

He was feeling a little light.

Where did the corn family put their Christmas presents?

In their stalk-ings

Why didn't the bells have dates?

Because they were Single Bells

What did the fruit salad say on December 25?

"Berry Christmas!"

What is a chicken's favorite holiday drink?

Eggnog

Why did the elves calendar have so many holes?

It was a vent calendar.

What did the elves say when they saw "Santa Caus" written on a letter?

Noel, Noel

What do Christmas presents like listening to?

Wrap music

What do you call a crab that gives presents?

Santa Claws

What stops an elf from stealing toys?

Santa Laws

What did the fire get for Christmas?

Two lumps of coal!

Why didn't the knight speak at Christmas?

He was a "Silent Knight"

What do all elves want for Christmas?

A day off!

What do you call leftover spaghetti on Christmas?

The Ghost of Christmas Pasta

What kind of cookies like going down hills?

Gingersled men

What's a nose's favorite Christmas song?

Jingle Smells

What's Santa's favorite seasoning?

Christmas Thyme

What is the reindeer's favorite board game?

Guess Hoof

What does a Christmas tree say when it goes to the bathroom?

I need to tinsel.

What's a snowman's favorite cereal?

Snow Flakes

Why didn't the man like Christmas Eve?

He had Claustrophobia

What did the salt say to the pepper on Christmas?

Seasoning's greetings!

What is Santa's favorite dance?

The ho-ho-hokie pokie.

Why did the calendar come with a free bell?

So you can ring in the new year!

What do you call a snowman covered in cake?

Frosting the Snowman

What did the snowman say when it got its eyes?

It's beginning to look a lot like Christmas.

What is Adam's favorite night?

Christmas Eve

MERRY CHRISTMAS!

Silly Jokes

How do eyeballs congratulate each other?

Eye five!

What do you get when you mix spaghetti and hotdogs with ice-cream and pickles?

Sick.

What makes Oscar the Grouch happy?

When his house is trashed.

What are a skunk's two favorite letters?

P.U.

How do you know when you're talking too much?

When you start interrupting yourself.

What does the UFO call his best friend?

Brother from another hover.

Why was Thor so tired of working out?

His arms were Thor, his legs were Thor, in fact, he was just Thor all over!

What does the haunted rooster say?

Cocka-doodle-BOO!

Why was Simba crowned king?

Because he was the mane man!

What did Woody say when Buzz Lightyear said he was a real astronaut?

"Are you toying with me?!"

What did Cogsworth the clock say when Mrs. Potts sang Tale as Old as Time?

"Who are you calling old?!"

What happened when the Beast fell ill?

He received Belle service!

Why was Pocahontas mad at Grandmother Willow?

Because she kept throwing shade!

Why didn't the royal artist make it into the castle?

Because he couldn't draw the bridge!

What did Sleeping Beauty say when the salesman tried to sell her a new bed?

"I'll have to sleep on it!"

What happened when the mascara the girl wanted wasn't available?

She lashed out!

What did the Mad Hatter say when he broke his teacup?

"I don't think I've got a handle on this!"

What did the girl wearing all black say to her date?

"I goth to go!"

Why couldn't Snow White fall in love with a doctor?

Because an apple a day keeps the doctor away!

How did Simba's lion family react when he was crowned king?

They roared with approval!

How did Cinderella's stepsisters get rid of the prince?

They shooed him away!

What did Sleeping Beauty think of the movie?

She couldn't stay awake!

What did the dragon say after the prince told him a funny joke?

"Haha! You slay me!"

What kind of kiss is the sweetest?

A Hershey's kiss!

What did Ariel say when she got tangled in seaweed?

"Kelp me!"

How does the story of Peter Pan end?

Happily never after!

What's the saddest thing in the ocean?

A blue whale

Are clams strong?

No, but mussels are.

What's it called when a skunk and a clove of garlic say their opinion?

They give their two scents.

What did the car do when it ran out of gas?

It took a brake.

What did the chickpeas say to the singer?

"Will you hummus a tune?"

Did you hear about the horse who had to go to the hospital?

He's in stable condition.

Where do ants like to go on vacation?

Antarctica

What did the bald eagle want for Christmas?

A toupee

What does a salesman say when he goes away?

Buy buy!

What does a vampire say when he doesn't like something?

"This bites."

Did you hear about the horse that did poorly on his paper?

He became a C-Horse

Where do cats keep their money?

Inside of their purrrrse.

What do you call a pig stuck in a bush?

A hedgehog

What is ice cream's favorite dance move?

The milkshake.

What's the most eco-friendly veggie?

A green bean

What do you call a sweet pea that went insane?

A peanut

What did the tiny bucket say before he fainted?

"I'm a little pail."

What does cheese say when it's happy?

"I feel grate!"

What type of bees do dogs love to catch?

Fris-bees.

How do you know when two spiders get married?

They tie the knot.

What do crocodiles cook with?

Crockpots!

What do dust bunnies use to cook their meals?

Dustpans!

What does a corn spider spin?

Cobwebs.

What does a cat in pain say?

"Me-OWW!"

What is a tree's favorite drink?

Root beer.

When the camel asked for sugar with his tea, what did the waitress ask?

"One hump or two?"

What did the dog say to the tree?

"Bark."

What did the doctor say to the person in the waiting room?

"Be patient!"

Why did the knight use poison instead of his sword to kill the mythical winged, fire-breathing creature?

He didn't want the fight to drag-on.

Why isn't "Werewolf" spelled with an "H"?

No one wants to scream "Herewolf"!

What's the best kind of paper to make a paper airplane out of?

Fly Paper.

What did Pinocchio say after making a deal with the fox?

"No strings attached!"

In what direction did Pocahontas point the lost traveler?

Just around the river bend!

What do you call a crowd full of puppies?

An awwdience

How did Rapunzel describe her new hair dryer?

"It didn't blow me away!"

What did the hippie say to the baby who hated vegetables?

Give peas a chance!

What do you call a snowman with nothing to do?

Snowbored

What do you call a triangle that saves your life?

A guardian angle.

What do trash cans like to eat?

Junk food

Which animal loves the Pansy flower?

Chimpanzee!

The Bearded Lady from the circus went to the pet store to buy a pet. What did she buy?

A bearded dragon.

What do you call it if it's so cold your tears freeze?

Eye-sickles.